START S.M.A.R.T.

Use S.M.A.R.T. Goals to Achieve More, Get What You Want, and Turn Your Dreams into Reality

JUSTIN BYERS

© Copyright 2013 by Empowerment Nation - All rights reserved.

This publication is designed to provide accurate and authoritative information in regard to the subject matter covered. It is sold with the understanding that the publisher is not engaged in rendering legal, accounting or other professional services. If legal advice or other professional assistance is required, the services of a competent professional person should be sought.

- From a Declaration of Principles jointly adopted by a Committee of the American Bar Association and a Committee of Publishers and Associations.

All rights reserved. No part of this publication may be reproduced or transmitted in any form or by any means, electronic or mechanical, including photocopy, recording, or any information storage or retrieval system, without permission in writing from the publisher.

No responsibility or liability is assumed by the Publisher for any injury, damage or financial loss sustained to persons or property from the use of this information, personal or otherwise, either directly or indirectly. While every effort has been made to ensure reliability and accuracy of the information within, all liability, negligence or otherwise, from any use, misuse or abuse of the operation of any methods, strategies, instructions or ideas contained in the material herein, is the sole responsibility of the reader.

Any copyrights not held by publisher are owned by their respective authors.

All information is generalized, presented for informational purposes only and presented "as is" without warranty or guarantee of any kind.

All trademarks and brands referred to in this book are for illustrative purposes only, are the property of their respective owners and not affiliated with this publication in any way. Any trademarks are being used without permission, and the publication of the trademark is not authorized by, associated with or sponsored by the trademark owner.

EmpowermentNation.com

Table of Contents

Introduction 1
    How to Use This Book 3
Why Goal-Setting? 7
    Achieve More with Your Time 8
    Feel More Fulfilled and Satisfied 12
Identifying Your Goals 14
    Defining Success 15
    Focusing on Fulfillment 19
    Visualizing the Future 24
    Writing a Roadmap to the Future 28
Making Your Goals S.M.A.R.T. Goals 36
    Specific 36
    Motivated 39
    Achievable 41
    Realistic 43
    Time-Targeted 46
    S.M.A.R.T. Goals Checklist 48
Strategies for Starting and Completing Your Goals 51
    Goal Journal 52
    To-Do Lists 55
    Creating Vision Boards 59
    Accountability Partners 61
    Goal Reminders 66

- Rewards System 68
- Overcoming Roadblocks 72
  - Staying Focused on Your Goals 72
  - Forgiving Yourself 75
  - Adapting Goals to Changes 78
- Conclusion 82

<u>Introduction</u>

Have you ever taken a road trip? If you have, you know that the most memorable and important part of the trip is sometimes not the destination, but the route you take to get there and the planning that goes into making your trip run smoothly.

Planning and achieving a goal works the same way. When most of us think about our goals, we think about the end points: the day we get the promotion or lose twenty pounds or buy a new car. But if you want to actually achieve your goal, you have to do more than just fantasize about the day you achieve it. The day you achieve your goal is actually less important than all the days you spend in the process. Think of achieving your goals as being like taking a road trip. While there may be many miles to cover before you reach your destination, traveling those miles can be just as important, insightful, and maybe even fun as the end destination.

First, you have to figure out where you want to go. You might know already that you want to go to California, or maybe you have some sense that you want to go to a place with a warm climate or with mountains. Maybe you have no clue where you want to go, but you just know you need to move on from where you are. The same can be true of your goals. You might know exactly what you hope to achieve, or you might have some sense of what you want your life to be like, but you also might not really know what you want to do or be. That's okay. This book can help you first figure out what direction you're headed and then what your destination will be.

Once you know where you're going, you can plan your route. You can decide where to spend the night, what attractions to see along the way, and which roads will be best suited to your needs. Again, the same is true for your goals. Once you know what you want to achieve, you can make a roadmap of the steps you will take to achieve your goal. This book will help you break your big goals down into more manageable steps and make sure that your goals are written in a way that makes them achievable.

After all this planning is done, you can finally set off on your journey, knowing that you have a trusty roadmap to guide you. Once you start driving, you have to keep fuel in your tank and make sure you stay motivated to keep cruising down the road. Maybe you need to pack some CDs so you don't get bored or find a co-pilot to keep you company. This book can help you find similar ways to keep you motivated on your journey towards achieving your goals. We explain how you can find some company on the road, keep yourself motivated, and maintain a healthy pace so you get to your destination on time.

Finally, even after all this planning, sometimes an unexpected roadblock can send you on a detour, or a flat tire can force you off the road for a day or two. Worse, your transmission could die and send you back to where you started. Similarly, life obstacles, small or large, can get in the way of you achieving your goals. This book can give you the strategies you need to get back on your route or help you plan a new route if the old one becomes uncrossable.

No matter where you are starting and where you want to go, this book can help you make it to your destination, while also learning to appreciate the scenery and solitude of the road towards that destination.

How to Use This Book

If you are looking for comprehensive advice about discovering, setting, and pursuing your goals, you will want to read this book straight through from the beginning. However, if you have prior experience with goal-setting guides, but need help with a particular aspect of goal-setting or achieving your goals, you may want to start in the section most targeted to your needs.

It may also be useful to know exactly what each chapter of this book is going to teach you before you get started. This section will explain the purpose of each chapter in this book:

- *Why Goal-Setting?*: The first section of this book offers an exploration of the benefits of adopting a goal-setting system. Nobody needs to be persuaded to want to follow their dreams, but this section will explain to you the benefits of using this book and our recommended system for developing and working towards your goals.
- *Identifying Your Goals*: This section is especially useful if you know you want to make a change in your life, but you're not sure where to start or how to clarify what it is you want. For some people, identifying your goals is easy, but for many of us, just figuring out what we want is half the battle. The exercises in this section will help you determine what success looks like for you and what your ideal future will look like, which will help you determine what your goals are and how to achieve them.
- *Making Your Goals S.M.A.R.T. Goals*: If you have tried to set and achieve goals previously, but have failed, this section will probably help. This section details the traits good goals should have. It's possible that your goal-setting efforts have previously faltered because your

goals didn't meet these crucial guidelines. For those of you just getting started with goal-setting, this section will explain the importance of making your goals specific, motivated, achievable, realistic, and time-targeted.
- *Strategies for Starting and Completing Your Goals*: This section is important for everyone, as it details how to put your goals into action using a variety of tools and methods. If you know you have struggled with achieving your goals in the past, even if you have adhered to S.M.A.R.T. guidelines or other goal-setting advice, this section may help you find a way to take more successful action towards achieving your goals.
- *Overcoming Roadblocks*: The final main section of this book will explain how to keep going with your goals even when life throws some obstacles in your way. This section is important for everyone, as life can be unpredictable and make completing your goals challenging. If you know you have been blown off course from your goals by an unexpected change of circumstances previously, this section can help you be sure to adapt to any similar setbacks in the future.

You should feel free to jump into

whatever section sounds most interesting to you right away, but reading the book straight through will walk you through the steps needed to make a comprehensive action plan and start working towards your goals today.

Why Goal-Setting?

If you have found your way to this book, you are probably already persuaded that developing a goal-setting plan will help you transform your life and achieve your dreams. But you may be wondering why these particular methods for achieving your goals are going to be the best. It is true that you will have to put in some work as you figure out what your goals are, develop plans to achieve them, and then start working towards them.

However, all the work you put in to setting your goals and starting to move towards them will have an immense payoff. Following the steps outlined in this book will help you develop a comprehensive action plan for achieving each of your goals and will help you re-orient your life so that your goals become the primary focus. Achieving your goals is a benefit in and of itself, but learning goal-setting skills will also help you to achieve more with your time, to lead a more productive life, and to feel more fulfilled and happy with yourself and your life.

Think back to the analogy of taking a road trip. The more planning you do ahead of time, the more smoothly your trip will go once you're on the road. The same is true for setting your goals: the more work you put in to the planning stage, the more successful you will be.

Achieve More with Your Time

Having an action plan for your goals will help you get more done and work more productively. How many times have you gotten through your whole day only to realize that you didn't get done what you meant to or needed to? Instead you may have spent your time distracted by temporary problems or else wasting your time on pointless tasks. Developing an action plan for your goals can help prevent that sinking feeling from setting in.

With more technological advances coming day by day, distraction is a mere swipe of the finger away. For many of us, e-mail, Facebook, and text messaging provide a constant stream of distractions and attractions. If you're not paying attention, sometimes it can feel like you spend the whole day responding to messages, phone calls, and e-mails. Although some of this constant communication may involve productive tasks relating to work, school, or family, communication devices can make it difficult to focus on other things you have to get done. The danger is that this constant frenzy of communication creates a feeling of false busyness. You aren't getting anything done and yet it feels like you have no free time.

Even if you aren't inundated with incoming communication, you still undoubtedly find yourself dealing with distractions on a daily basis. The call of the dishwasher, the laundry pile, and the checkbook—all tasks that do admittedly need doing—keeps us from spending our time achieving our goals. You may feel like you are working all day but never getting anything done, because most of your energy is dedicated to these maintenance tasks that never add up to positive change or advancement.

One way to break out of this bad habit is to have a list of goals and tasks you need to achieve, so that you can re-prioritize your energies. If you know you have to do some specific research or go to the gym or finish drafting a business plan on a given day, you will be better able to avoid becoming distracted by unimportant things. Instead, you can make sure you prioritize completing your goal-related tasks. Maybe you can leave some e-mails to be responded to later. Or maybe you realize that you don't actually have to do that load of laundry; instead you can ask someone else to do it. Having other goals to work on can also help motivate you to get through things like housework or responding to communication more quickly, as you know you have other, better things to be spending your time on.

Having specific tasks to work on each day also helps you use your free time or time at work more productively. I know that if I don't set up some specific tasks for my day, I am likely to spend too much time watching TV, surfing the web, or doing some other mindless activity. If, however, I start my day with a list of things to do, I am likely to get those things done. Having a constant list of tasks can keep you from falling into a mindless game of Solitaire while at work or prevent you from frittering away your lunch break reading a magazine.

Having a list of tasks is also helpful for those times when you are most tempted to simply veg out. At the end of the day or on the weekend after a long week, you might be too tired to think about what else you want or need to get done. But if you have a list of productive tasks at the ready, you can probably muster enough energy to complete a task, even if it is something small. You just need that list to be created in advance, and then you will be able to use your time more productively and keep positive momentum rolling towards achieving your goals. I know that when I was trying to establish healthier eating habits, I would sometimes find it really difficult to find the energy to cook a healthy dinner at the end of the day, especially if I had to come up with an idea for something to eat. However, if I had a list of healthy recipes at the ready and some ingredients stocked up in the fridge, I could manage to find the time and energy to put together a healthy meal. I just had to do a little planning ahead.

Try it Now: To see this benefit of goal-setting in action, try making a little list of goal-related tasks that you can complete tomorrow or today. These should be things that you could realistically work into your day and get done. Make a list of 3-5 tasks you can complete by the end of the day today or tomorrow. At this point, you may just be getting started with goal-setting and might not be sure of what your long-term goals are. That's okay. If this is the case, your tasks might include reading more of this book and completing one of the activities outlined in later chapters. At the end of the day, reflect on how you managed to find time to complete these tasks. Were you able to get through some other tasks more quickly to make time for your goal tasks? Did you find a pocket of time that would normally have gone to waste?

One of the biggest differences between successful, productive people and people who are unable to achieve their goals is how these two types of people use their time. The successful person uses every available window of time to accomplish something goal-oriented, while the person who is still struggling is probably spending too much time on needless tasks or on time-wasters. Establishing what your goals are and then creating lists of tasks for achieving these goals will help you become a member of that first group, someone who is always focused on the big picture and the future.

Feel More Fulfilled and Satisfied

If you found your way to this book about goal-setting, you are probably experiencing some level of dissatisfaction or unhappiness with your life or yourself. You might feel discouraged and far away from your dreams, or you might feel frustrated with your own inability to get things done. Developing a concrete plan for your future and for every day leading up to that future will help you feel more fulfilled and satisfied with your life.

Many of us don't give ourselves enough credit for the hard work we do every day. Instead, we focus too much on the failures and shortcomings of each day. I know that at the end of the day it can be hard for me to acknowledge what I may have accomplished, because I am thinking instead about what I still need to do, or what I will need to accomplish tomorrow. But if I have a to-do list for the day or for the week, even if I fall a little behind, I'm able to see how much good work I have put into my life that week and focus on gratitude and positive self-esteem. Having a system of assigned daily tasks that you can cross off of a list will help you to keep in mind all that you have achieved and to develop a more positive outlook.

With this more positive attitude and increased focus on your goals also comes more successes to feel good about. Without any particular plan in mind, it's easy to spend a day on pointless tasks or on distractions that come between us and our goals. This can lead to increased self-criticism and negative attitudes. When you aren't getting much done towards achieving your goals, you aren't going to feel that great about yourself. But if you know you are taking small steps towards your goals every single day, you will feel happier and more fulfilled with your life, even well before you actually reach the point of achieving your goals.

Even if you are still some distance from achieving your ultimate goals, waking up each day with a sense of purpose because you have at least identified those goals and the steps you need to take to achieve them will help improve your life. When you know what you are working towards in the future, it is easier to accept less than ideal circumstances in the present. Developing a goal-setting plan can help you feel happier and more fulfilled even before you achieve your goals, because you will start each day with a sense of purpose and direction that will otherwise be missing from your life.

Identifying Your Goals

For many of us, one of the hardest parts of setting and achieving our goals is identifying exactly what those goals are. You probably came to this book because of a sense that you want to make a change in your life or because of a feeling of dissatisfaction. You might have some idea of what you want your future to hold, but that vision of the future may be a little hazy. You might also be struggling with realizing that your goals and dreams don't necessarily line up with what society has told you to want or expect for your whole life. This chapter will help you identify your own individual goals, and start to make a plan to make them happen.

Even if you have come to this book with a pretty clear sense of what goals you want to achieve, you will still benefit from clarifying those goals through the activities outlined in this section. You also might discover through some of these activities that your stated goals don't line up with the motivations behind them. Maybe you think you have a goal of earning more money, when really what you want is to be able to travel or support your family. Maybe you have clear career goals but aren't sure what you want to happen in your personal life. This chapter can help you clarify and identify goals for all aspects of your life.

This chapter will help you define success

on your own terms and select goals based on what will make you truly happy and fulfilled. This chapter will also help you discover what your goals are and break those goals into steps that you can begin to take action on right away. This important groundwork will set you up for future success, by helping you develop a better sense of who you are and what you want.

When setting out on your road trip, choosing a destination and a direction is obviously an important first step. This chapter can help you make sure you don't go all the way to California when what you want is a beach, which could be found closer to home. This chapter can also help you make sure you don't choose to go to Florida just because Florida is popular with your friends or family. This chapter will help you identify where you want to go, whether that's Montana or France, based on your own unique interests, needs, and desires.

Defining Success

Success is an impossibly broad word. What one person deems a success, another person may call a total failure. Success in one part of your life might not translate to success in another. So how can you achieve success or call yourself successful without knowing exactly what success is? When it comes to setting goals and envisioning your future, one of the first steps you must take is figuring out what success means to you.

Our culture gives us many ideas about what success is supposed to look like: a big house, a fancy car, an attractive husband or wife, a high-paying and powerful job. TV and the media promote this version of "success" above most others, and many of us have been on the track towards achieving these goals for a long time. Many of us go right from high school to whatever job pays best. Or right from high school to college, where we major in something that will make money, not necessarily something that will make us happy. After college, we take the best job we can find and devote ourselves to working our way up the ladder, no matter whether this career is fulfilling or not. Maybe we get married, buy a house, and have kids, and then expect happiness to be waiting for us.

Instead, often, we find ourselves dissatisfied. Our lack of fulfilment with the direction our lives are heading catches up to us, and we find ourselves wishing we could find something that would make us truly happy. True happiness comes from feeling like a success. And while the main goals of society may make some of us happy, success achieved on your own terms will be far more meaningful and lead to far greater happiness.

So what does success mean for you? Do you want to feel like you are making a difference in the world? Do you want to have a happy, healthy family? Do you want to have time to travel and enjoy your leisure time? Do you want to create something meaningful? Do you want to become a master at something?

Here's the thing: you don't need to pursue anything that doesn't fit into your own, personal definition of success. Even if it seems like everyone around you is pressuring you to live your life a certain way, the only way you will be happy is if you achieve success on your own terms. So forget about the fancy car, the big house, and the big-name job, and think about what would be fulfilling to you.

(Goal setting worksheets are available to assist you with exercises both in this chapter and throughout the rest of the book. You can either fill them out on your computer or print them for your convenience. Download them at http://empowermentnation.com/downloads/38/GoalsettingWorksheet.pdf)

> **Try It Now:** Let's paint a picture of what success looks like to you. Imagine that you have reached old age, even past retirement age, and are reflecting on your life. Don't think about your present day worries or troubles. Just imagine that you are looking back on the life you are currently living. What do you want to

have done? What do you want your legacy to be? What do you want to have left behind? Write this as a short paragraph or make a list of three to five things you hope you will have achieved and what your picture of success looks like. Below are several examples.

Example One: I hope that I have made time for my family. I hope that I have provided security and stability for my children, but, more than that, I hope that I have been there for them through their whole lives. I also hope that I have lived a long, healthy life by maintaining an active lifestyle and quitting smoking. I hope that I stay healthy so I can be involved in my children's lives into my old age.

Example Two: I hope that I did something that leaves a meaningful impact on my community. I hope that I worked hard to make a positive change in the lives of the people around me. I also hope that I pursued my dream of learning to play music and making my love of music a bigger part of my life.

Example Three: I hope that I grew my own successful business that can become something I can leave behind for my family. I hope that I can constantly surround myself with positive people and influences who support me and form a community. I also hope that I write the book I have always wanted to write.

Do you see how these visions of success all differ, based on individual desires and dreams? And none of them actually fit that standard model of "success" that is based mostly on material possessions. To take care of your family, make a meaningful change in a community, or grow a successful business, you don't have to sell your soul to a demanding career. And a house with a three-car garage and a pair of BMWs isn't going to make any of these people happy, because these material possessions are just not necessary to their visions of success.

So now that you have determined your own vision of success—what you ultimately hope to achieve in your life—let's talk about how to make that dream a reality.

Focusing on Fulfillment

In the process of figuring out your vision of success, you were not thinking about what other people expect of you, but about what would make you feel *fulfilled.* Fulfilment is a feeling of satisfaction you get when you are pleased with what you have achieved.

The feeling of fulfilment can't be faked. Almost certainly, there have been times in your life when you have "achieved" something other people thought of as a good thing, but that didn't mean much to you. Maybe you went to college because your family forced you to, so you didn't feel very fulfilled by graduating. Maybe you got a promotion, even though you were happier at your old job. Maybe you bought a huge, beautiful home but in a neighborhood far from your family. Even though people around you might have been offering their congratulations, you were not happy because these accomplishments really did not satisfy your desires.

On the other hand, there have undoubtedly been times in your life when you have felt fulfilled. Maybe you love helping others, and so even something as simple as helping a family member hang a shelf or explaining how to do something at work makes you feel fulfilled. Maybe you feel fulfilled when you volunteer at church or school or when you were able to work for a non-profit making positive change in your community. Maybe you just feel most fulfilled when you are at the dinner table with your family.

If you aren't sure what gives you the greatest fulfillment in your life, don't worry. The following exercises will help you identify the things that give you fulfillment, so that you can re-organize your life to pursue more sources of fulfillment.

> **Try It Now:** The following exercises should help you locate your sources of fulfillment. For these exercises, you'll need a notebook or several sheets of loose leaf paper, plus a pen or pencil. You should write continuously for the specified amount of time, letting whatever thoughts come into your head flow onto the page without judgment.
>
> *Exercise One:* For five minutes, brainstorm a list of times in your adult life (not childhood) when you have felt most happy and fulfilled. Just start by listing experiences that seemed meaningful to you at the time and that made you feel a feeling of fullness or fulfilment. Don't judge any of the items that come out during this listing process; the point is to let your mind wander and consider even small moments that might have left a lasting impact. It can help to work backwards or forwards systematically over time, going from past to present or present to past. Think through various jobs you have held, volunteer experiences you may have had,

and also smaller, more personal experiences or tasks.

Exercise Two: Once you have created a list of fulfilling experiences, jobs, or tasks, look over this list and choose two or three that seem especially significant. For each of these, you should complete the following exercise. For five minutes, focus on the experience you found fulfilling. Write a description of what you did, including sensory details like how things looked, smelled, sounded, etc. Now describe the feeling of fulfillment you got from this experience. What did fulfillment feel like? How did you feel while completing the task? How did you feel after? What was the best part of this experience? What was the most difficult part? What parts do you remember most vividly to this day?

Exercise Three: Now that you have explored in greater detail several fulfilling experiences, you should be able to identify what kinds of general activities or processes make you feel fulfilled. You should summarize your fulfilling experiences in a way that finishes out the sentence "I feel most fulfilled when..." You might feel most fulfilled when helping others, when spending time around loved ones, when using your writing skills, when acting as a leader, etc. Whatever it is, try to boil down your fulfilling experiences to a couple of general activities or traits. You may never be able to do exactly what you did to feel fulfilled in the past, but this step will help you identify what the true source of your feeling of fulfilment is.

Once you have completed these exercises, you should be able to clearly identify what it is that makes you feel fulfilled and what tasks or experiences have given you that feeling in the past. It is crucial that you not judge yourself or think of yourself as being less important based on what kinds of things have given you a feeling of fulfilment in the past. You may be realizing that the moments you have felt most fulfilled are not the kinds of moments most people are told are important to pursue. This doesn't matter. Whatever experiences make you feel most fulfilled, however big or small, are those you should focus on moving towards so that you will feel satisfied, happy, and successful.

Once you have figured out what your sources of fulfilment are, you can start to think about what kinds of experiences you should pursue to find more of that feeling in the future.

Visualizing the Future

Now that you have thought about what success looks like and determined your sources of fulfillment, you have probably started to think about what the future will look like once you start trying to achieve your version of success and fulfillment. This section will help you envision your goals and the future, so that you can make your goals become a reality.

Visualizing your goals has a powerful benefit of helping you believe that your goals can come true. Sometimes, when we think about our goals, we think about them so that it seems like they are happening to some other person in some distant life. But visualizing your goals happening to you, in the life you are already living, will start to make them feel more real and achievable. Also, if you simply think of your goals in an abstract way, not connected with your current, daily life, you will have a hard time knowing how to achieve them or even when you have achieved them. You want to have a clear picture of what your ideal life looks like, so you can help make that life become a reality.

Visualizing your future can also help you clarify your goals. Again, you might be thinking of your goals in an abstract way not all that connected with your current daily life, so these goals might not be realistic and might not even be what you actually want. You might think you want to be a millionaire, but when you really try to envision your life with the kind of job you'd need to become a millionaire, you realize that this is a hollow dream and not an actual goal based on what will make you feel fulfilled. Imagining what the ideal version of your life looks like can help you figure out what goals are most important to you and what you really hope to achieve.

> **Try it Now:** To complete this exercise, you will need some paper and a writing utensil or else your computer and a word processing program.

To start, you should write a detailed description of a day in your life ten years from now. Take yourself through the whole day, with descriptions of each part. Try to make it feel like a diary entry from your life in the future. Start with waking up: Where do you live? Do you have a family? What is your house like? Do you have pets? What is the feeling in the space where you live? Then take us through a work day, whatever that might look like. Think about your ideal job or career and walk us through what you spend each day doing in that life: Do you work from home or in an office? Do you own a business? Do you have a different career than you do in your life now? What is your work environment like? What tasks do you spend most of your time doing? Then walk us through how you spend your time outside of work: What hobbies do you pursue? What is your social life like? What are your health habits? Who do you spend your time with? And then, think about what you reflect on at the end of the day: How do you feel about your life? What is the feeling you get at the end of each day? How do you cope with hardships that may come your way?

Then, you should repeat this exercise completely, this time thinking of what kind of life you will have *five* years from now. This vision should be kind of a halfway point between your life now and your life ten years from now. Maybe in ten years you hoped to own and run a successful business, so five years from now maybe that business is just starting out. Maybe you saw yourself living in a large home ten years from now, so five years from now you should see yourself saving money. But do exactly the same exercise, thinking through each aspect of your day five years in the future.

Now, again, repeat the same exercise for your life *one* year from now. Now you have to be somewhat realistic about what you can change or achieve in one year, but really consider what you hope your life looks like in one year. What steps will you have to have made a year from now to put you closer to achieving your ten-year dream? As before, write this like a diary entry that covers your whole day.

Now, although this might sound crazy, you're going to do the same thing but for a day in your life starting *tomorrow*. You can't say you'll have a new job or have gotten married or have moved to a new place. But what changes could you make in your daily life that would put you better on track for your future? What kind of day in your life would make you feel fulfilled? What does an ideal day look like in the life you are already living? Again, write this out like a diary entry, walking through each part of your day.

Once you have completed this task of visualizing your life at various points in the future, you should have greater clarity about the things that are important to you and what your goals are. Ideally, you should also have thought about a range of things you hope to accomplish or change in your life, from small things to big things. Maybe you realized that you really want to have a dog, or change the way you dress, or live in a house that gets a lot of light. Those things are goals you could conceivably achieve right away and that would contribute to your fulfilment. You also surely visualized parts of your life that will require greater time and energy to change, but this book can help you outline a plan to make even those big, intimidating changes happen.

Writing a Roadmap to the Future

Now that you have established what your future will look like, you want to narrow in on a few specific goals and figure out how to achieve them. For the purpose of this section, you will want to pick one of the goals you want to achieve based on one of your vision exercises. You should repeat this road-mapping exercise with each goal, but you should take them one at a time.

One of the biggest roadblocks we encounter when it comes to achieving our goals is failing to translate big-picture dreams into the smaller steps needed to achieve them. Focusing on the end result—when you will achieve your goal—can help you stay motivated, but you won't even be able to get started on achieving your goals without figuring out what steps you have to take first to achieve them.

To break a large goal into more manageable steps, start by breaking the large goal down into "way stations," smaller goals that can be achieved along the way. Think of your ultimate goal as being your ultimate destination in the road trip and these smaller goals as rest stops or landmarks, places where you can take satisfaction in having achieved your goal part of the way.

For some goals, the way station goals will be building blocks towards achieving the ultimate goal. If you want to become a nurse, maybe you first need to score well on college admissions tests, then apply and be accepted to a nursing program, then complete your degree, and then find a job. In this case, you can't skip a step or go out of order, but each task is a significant one you should reward yourself for. For other goals, however, your way stations may be milestones that you put in place to keep you motivated, but they may not need to be stacked on top of each other. For example, if your goal is to lose ten pounds in three months, you might set way station goals of giving up fast food for a month, losing half of your goal weight, and being able to jog a mile. You could do those tasks in a variety of different orders, but they all are significant achievements that help you along the way to your ultimate goal. Each way station goal does not necessarily lead directly to the next, but they are arranged in a way that they get a little more challenging as they go, and completing one will help you complete the next.

There is no right or wrong way to break your specific goals down into these way stations, as each goal will be slightly different. For a goal that you expect to achieve in about one year, you should have at least 5-6 way station goals that you can plan to achieve every other month or so. Longer-term goals will require more planning and breaking down into steps, while shorter-term goals may be simpler to break down.

Once you have established your way stations, you want to think about what smaller tasks you will need to achieve each month, week, and day to work towards those goals. Try to break each way station goal into as many small tasks as possible. These small tasks will seem easier to achieve than the large way station goal, which helps you get going right away. In the above examples, you could write a list of things you can do to prepare for taking and studying for college admissions examinations or steps you can take each day to make sure that you are successful in giving up fast food for the month.

You should break your main goal into an outline of way station goals and the steps required to achieve them, so that your page looks something like this:

Goal Action Plan

Main Goal:

Way Station Goals:

Outline of way station goals and sub goals, with deadlines for each step:

(You can also use our downloadable goal-setting worksheets as a template. If you have not already done so, you can download them at http://empowermentnation.com/downloads/38/GoalsettingWorksheet.pdf)

For example, you might fill it out like this:

Goal: In three months be ten pounds lighter and able to complete a 5K walking and jogging.
Way Station Goals: 1. Give up fast food for a month. 2. Reach five pounds lost. 3.

Be able to jog a mile.

Tasks:

1. First month: Give up fast food for the month.
    a. Research healthy eating in books from the library.
    b. Join a gym.
    c. Replace one unhealthy food I usually eat with one healthy food. (Yogurt and fruit for breakfast instead of bagels.)
    d. Spend one hour per week exercising.
    e. Learn to prepare five new healthy dinners.
2. Second month: Reach five pounds lost.
    a. Try a new class at the gym.
    b. Spend one and a half hours each week exercising.
    c. Prepare each of five healthy dinners learned last month twice.
    d. Replace one more unhealthy food I usually eat with a healthy alternative. (Salads for lunch instead of sandwiches.)
3. Third month: Be able to jog a mile.
    a. Spend two hours each week exercising.
    b. Sign up for a 5K race for next month.
    c. Establish habit of drinking six

glasses of water each day.
- d. Replace another unhealthy food with a healthy alternative. (Fruit and organic frozen yogurt instead of ice cream for dessert.)
- e. Learn three new healthy dinners to prepare.

At the end of these three months, I should be able to complete my 5K and also should have lost weight. Do you notice how each of the sub-goals becomes more complicated or difficult each month? The amount of exercise increases month to month, and healthy foods are implemented gradually, rather than all at once. I also tried to think of sub-goals for each month that would be easy to achieve, but that would be on track for the overall goal, such as trying a new class at the gym or signing up for a 5K. Having some variety built in to your goals also keeps you from stagnating or getting burned out. It takes some creativity and careful thinking to work out a detailed plan like this, but this is the best way to be sure you stay on track for the whole three months and come out slimmer and fitter.

If you feel overwhelmed at this stage, it may be because the first step towards achieving your goals is actually research. If you think back to the metaphor of setting out on a road trip towards your goal, don't forget that there is a lot of work that has to go into preparing for that journey. Before you can plan your route, you need to research the possibilities and find out what routes other people have used on similar journeys. If you are still in the preparation stage, don't let this discourage you from pursuing your goals. Simply make research a part of your action plan.

For example, let's say you want to open a restaurant in your area, but you don't really know where to start. Your first goals might look something like this:

1. Research starting a restaurant.
    a. Find books at the library about opening a small business or restaurant.
    b. Read five books and take notes on the strategies they suggest.
    c. Reach out to three successful local restaurant owners and ask to interview them.
    d. Research new restaurants opening and scheduled to open in my town.
2. Create a detailed goal plan for opening a restaurant.
    a. Determine financial requirements and start-up costs.
    b. Determine timeline for opening a restaurant.

      c.   Determine market and style of restaurant.
      d.   Determine location and size of restaurant.

Once you complete step one, you can achieve step two, which involves actually creating the rest of the many-step plan you will need to open a restaurant. Right now, step two just includes the elements that you should find the answers to in your research. Answering these questions will allow you to lay out a full action plan towards achieving this goal.

If you are in a similar circumstance and are unsure of how to go about pursuing a goal, it's okay to have an incomplete action plan for now. Instead, focus on making an action plan for researching your goal, approaching it from as many different perspectives as possible, and wait to make more detailed plans until you better understand the process.

Creating this roadmap or action plan is one of the most important steps you can take towards achieving your goals. A detailed plan can make a goal that seems difficult or overwhelming seem suddenly achievable. With this action plan, you will know not only where you are going, but also how you will get there.

__Making Your Goals S.M.A.R.T. Goals__

As you create your action plan, there are a few things you should keep in mind to make sure that you will be able to achieve your goals. To make sure that your goals are goals that you can succeed in achieving, you should make sure that each goal and way station goal adheres to some certain traits. There are lots of different guidelines and suggestions out there for setting good goals. One of the most popular is the acronym S.M.A.R.T. This acronym tells you that your goals should be all of the following things:

- Specific
- Motivated
- Achievable
- Realistic
- Time-Targeted

This section will explain in detail what each of these adjectives means in relation to your goals. Making sure your goals follow these guidelines will mean your goals are more likely to be achieved.

Specific

As we have already discussed somewhat in earlier sections, it is crucial that your goals be as specific as possible. Vague, broad goals are almost impossible to achieve both because they are too big and because they are too loosely defined.

Many of us tend to naturally think in terms of broad, vague goals. You might say to yourself "I want to be happy" or "I want to be successful" or "I want to be rich." While those might all be true statements, they are also very vague. It is difficult to say exactly you might mean by "happy" or "successful" or "rich." As explained in the "Defining Success" section earlier, there are so many definitions of success that one person's version of success can be radically different from another person's. The same is true of words like "happy" or "rich." These vague, abstract concepts make it so your goals are constantly elusive, seeming always just beyond your grasp.

Not only are these broad goals too difficult to define, they are too huge to be focused on. Because they are so broad, they seem impossible to achieve. Does one day of feeling "happy" mean you have achieved your goal? How about a month? A week of happy days in a row? The lack of specificity in the goal makes it so you will never achieve it. Furthermore, lack of specificity means you have nowhere to start towards achieving your goal. If you want to be "successful," how do you get started? What is the first step towards a goal as broad as "success?"

Although you may start with a vague or broad sense of a goal when you are first brainstorming, it is crucial that you narrow down that goal. So while you may start with a broad goal like "I want to be rich," you have got to quantify that goal so that you can actually try to achieve it. A better goal would be something like "I want to earn X more dollars each month." Instead of, "I want to be happy," you might make your goal to change one thing in your life that makes you unhappy; maybe make it your goal to get a new job or to complain less about your current circumstances. Instead of "I want to be successful," you might make it your goal to get a promotion or open a business that earns a profit after five years.

These kinds of specific goals are far more narrowly defined, so you know exactly what you will need to do to consider your goal achieved. Also, don't those specific goals just sound more obtainable? Huge aims like "success" and "happiness" and "wealth" and "health" seem so large they are impossible to achieve. No matter how far away you might be from achieving a goal like "losing fifty pounds" or "getting a promotion," you can see that the end is in sight and what steps you will need to take to get started.

Motivated

If you set out to achieve a large goal and you want to actually achieve it, it is also important that you have an emotional motivation behind your pursuit of that goal. Identifying this motivation can also help you make your goals more targeted and specific.

Many of us can think of times when we have set out to achieve a goal only to make someone else happy or because we felt like we should do something. Maybe you tried to learn a skill for work, but your heart wasn't really in it. Or maybe you remember slogging through studying for a class you had no interest in. It is very difficult to achieve goals we don't care about on an emotional level, no matter how much they may "make sense" or "seem like a good idea."

The goals you are going to work towards from here on out should be those that have a strong emotional motivation behind them. This ties back in with the exercises earlier in this book that were meant to help you find your sources of fulfilment and pursue them. Goals you are working to achieve because they give you personal fulfillment will be the easiest to achieve. That said, sometimes wanting to make someone else happy or care for someone else can also be a good, if perhaps slightly less powerful, motivator. However, this desire to make someone else happy must be something that will make you happy as well. Your own sense of fulfilment will be the greatest motivator for achieving your goals.

So at this point, you should think about what it is that is motivating you to achieve your goals. For example, if your goal is "I want to earn X more dollars per month," there has to be an actual *reason* why you want to earn that money. Think about how achieving that goal will make you *feel*. What is it that you hope that money will help you do? Will it make you feel more secure? Will it help you provide your family? Concentrating on the feeling you will get when you achieve your goal can help you stay focused when the going gets tough.

Also, think about whether or not there might be an underlying motivation behind that goal that might actually be your goal in itself. Do you want to travel? Buy a house? Start a business? Once you identify the emotional motivation behind a goal, not only will you be more likely to achieve it, but you also might realize that your goal isn't what you thought it was. You don't need to be a millionaire to travel, and it might be more important to find a flexible job and start saving for a plane ticket than to focus on building a large savings account. If you want to own a home, you could focus your efforts on saving up for a down payment, or you could realize your dream in a different way by buying an affordable fixer-upper and channeling your energies into remodeling. If you want to start a business, maybe you can start sooner than you think by finding investors or partnering with someone. Thinking about your emotional motivation can help you figure out exactly what it is you hope to achieve. This can help make your goals more *specific* and more *realistic* by narrowing down exactly what it is that would give you fulfilment.

Your goals can meet all of the other criteria outlined in this section, but if there is no emotional core motivating you to achieve your goal, you will be unlikely to achieve it. Spend your time doing only what you know will make you feel happy and fulfilled, and you will be on your way to goal success.

Achievable

Going hand-in-hand with your goal being specific, your goal has to be achievable. This means that your goal has to be something that has a definite endpoint. Someone looking in from outside, from an objective standpoint, should be able to look at you and your goal and see whether you have achieved it or not. The endpoint of your goal should be clear from the outset.

A goal like "be rich and famous" isn't just a bad goal because it is not specific enough and probably not emotionally motivated; it's also a bad goal because it isn't achievable. At what point, exactly, do you know you're "rich" or "famous?" Your definition of those terms might change over time, or you might not be able to identify exactly when you have achieved your goal. A more achievable goal will also be more specific, like "earn X more dollars per month" or "create a blog that gets X hits per month by next year." These goals, while related to the original, un-achievable goals, are much more capable of being achieved. You or someone else could verify when you have achieved them.

To make a goal achievable, you also have to have some method of measuring your progress towards your goal. Some goals lend themselves to this very easily. Weight loss or other health-related goals can be measured by the number on the scale or the time you can last on the treadmill. Financial goals can be measured by the numbers in a bank account. If you want to write a book, the number of words or pages you have written can be your measurement of progress. But for many other kinds of goals, you'll want to create your own metric for measuring your progress.

This may be as simple as establishing your series of way station goals that you must achieve according to a specific time frame. Think of each of these mini-goals as being like another pound lost or another hundred dollars added to your savings account. These way station goals and progress points will allow you to measure your progress on achieving this goal over time. You may need to be a little creative, but any goal can be broken into a system of measuring success.

Without a way to measure your progress, it is easy to lose focus because it can feel like you are never getting any closer to achieving your goal. Furthermore, a goal that cannot be measured in any way is probably too vague and not achievable anyway. To make sure that you can succeed in your goal plans, be sure that your goal has a built-in achievable endpoint and has a system for measuring progress.

Realistic

Though your goals should definitely encourage you to push yourself, your goals should also be realistic. This of course ties in with the previous section about your goals being *achievable*; a goal that can't be completed is not worth setting. You must modify your goals to make sure they meet some realistic criteria.

First of all, you should set realistic goals based on your starting point that also take into account factors outside your control. For instance, if you want to get in shape, your goal should not be to join the Olympic running team next year unless you are already a rather advanced runner. If you are starting off as someone who is out of shape, a more reasonable goal would be to complete a 5K or a 10K next year. This goal could more reasonably be achieved.

Your goals should also not depend on strokes of luck or outside factors that are unpredictable. No matter how much you want to become a rock star or a millionaire, these goals probably aren't realistic. They depend just as much on outside luck—getting discovered or hitting the lottery or getting lucky on the stock market—as on your own hard work. Set your goals so that they are only based on your own abilities. A more realistic goal for those two desires would be to learn to play the guitar or start a band, for the one, and to start a business or invest a certain amount of money, for the other. These goals are almost completely within your control and therefore can be realistically achieved. While the other dreams may come true, you can't quite control them, so they're not worth setting your sights on. If you work hard enough at your band or at growing your business, those more unrealistic goals may come true along the way, but they shouldn't be your focus.

You should also be realistic as you are laying out your timelines about the amount of time you will have to dedicate to your goal. Try to budget steps out according to how long they will realistically take. If you know you only have an hour or two per day to dedicate to your goal, don't set milestones that would require you to work twice that many hours. Better to set realistic goals that you can achieve and build momentum, rather than getting frustrated with yourself for falling behind almost immediately.

Your timelines should also be healthy and take into account your past progress. With health-related goals or weight-loss related goals, you want to push yourself, but you don't want to cause an injury. With other goals, be realistic about the amount of time or money you have to dedicate to each task. If you are staying up half the night just to get your goals completed on time, you are not creating a sustainable situation. While the push to achieve your goals should be motivating, it should not become a stressful burden that takes a toll on your health or wellbeing or that interferes with other important parts of your life.

If your goals are not realistic in any of the ways described above, you are setting yourself up for failure and burn-out. When people fail to achieve their goals, it's not because they don't want them enough, but because they go about trying to achieve them in the wrong way. Being unrealistic is one of the most deadly mistakes you can make when it comes to achieving your goals. If, on the second day, you are already exhausted and behind, you will just feel like giving up. Keep your goals realistic and manageable, however, and you'll be on your way to success.

Time-Targeted

Another important aspect of setting your goals is making sure you have a timeline for completing them. Without deadlines for achieving your way station goals and your main goal, you run the risk of losing motivation and failing to complete your goals.

Think about a time when someone asked you to do something for them or you set out to try to do something, but you didn't have a particular deadline. This could be anything from teaching a friend to use a computer program to studying Spanish. With no deadline to complete either of these tasks, you probably ignored them or kept putting them off for a time when you would really feel like doing them or have more time to do them. And then all of a sudden months went by and you still hadn't completed your goal. No matter how simple the goal might be, if you have no deadline to complete it, you will likely let it fall by the wayside.

The other important reason to keep your goals time-targeted is that your goals may change over time. If you set a goal for yourself and then don't achieve it, you may never return to this goal because your needs and priorities will have changed. This doesn't at all mean that that original goal wasn't worth pursuing; it probably was, but you missed out on the window where it made sense to achieve it.

This is especially important for goals that take a time commitment. If you want to go back to school, for example, and hope to earn a certificate or a new degree, you want to do so when the timing makes sense with whatever is going on in the rest of your life. If you set a specific, time-targeted goal right now to graduate with your certificate in two years, you will probably do it. If you set an open-ended goal to "go back to school eventually" you might not get it done quickly, and then you might never do it. Your family situation could start to demand more of your time, or a promotion at work could keep you from taking night classes. Or you might just give up on the goal because you feel like it has passed you by. You might be thinking, "well, I guess I didn't really need to do that anyway," but you probably know in your heart of hearts that going back to school would have helped you grow personally and professionally. Now you will have to find that growth some other way. If you set a specific timeline for completing this goal, you would be sure to complete it before your situation changes.

So, you must establish clear and specific timelines for achieving your goals. Give yourself a deadline for goal completion and for all your major way station goals along the way. Although you can be somewhat flexible, it is important to have a realistic timetable in mind when you begin your goal so that you are motivated to complete it.

S.M.A.R.T. Goals Checklist

To make sure that your goals adhere to the five traits of S.M.A.R.T. goals, you should work through the following checklist, answering each question in detail. Make sure that you have taken into account all aspects of S.M.A.R.T. goals for each of your goals. Working through this checklist can help you refine your goals and ensure that they will be successful. You'll also find these in the included worksheet, which you can download here: http://empowermentnation.com/downloads/38/GoalsettingWorksheet.pdf.

Specific
- Does my goal have any abstract, concept words (e.g. "success," "happiness," etc.) that can be replaced with more specific words?
- Are all the terms of my goal clearly defined?
- Does my goal focus on a specific aspect of a larger goal?
- Can my goal be broken down into any smaller parts?

Motivated
- How will I feel when I have completed my goal?
- What will achieving this goal allow me to do?
- Is my goal connected to one of my sources of fulfilment identified earlier?
- Should my goal be adapted to match the emotional motivation behind it?

Achievable
- Does my goal have a built-in endpoint?
- Could someone objectively evaluate when my goal has been completed?
- What is my system for measuring my progress towards achieving my goal?

Realistic
- What past goals or achievements have I based my goal off of?
- Is the success of my goal completely or mostly within my own control?
- Is my goal pushing or challenging me? Even if it is, can I achieve my goal in a healthy, realistic way?
- Are my goals sustainable over a long period of time?

Time-Targeted
- Have I established a deadline for

completing my goal?
- Have I assigned deadlines for each of the way station goals?
- How much time will it take out of each week to work towards completing this goal?
- Is my timeline achievable and realistic based on how much time I have to dedicate to this goal?
- What is my window of opportunity for completing this goal?

Strategies for Starting and Completing Your Goals

Now that you have decided on goals, created your action plan, and made sure that your goals are S.M.A.R.T. goals, you should be ready to start making progress towards actually achieving your goals. In the road trip analogy, this is the part where you actually get behind the wheel and start driving. If you have attempted to achieve a big goal before, you might know that this step, while it sounds simple, can actually be quite difficult. There are two main, if similar, difficulties you may face when getting started on a new goal. This section will help you tackle both.

First, it can be difficult to stay focused on your goals. You might put a lot of work into outlining your action plan, but if you don't stick to it, it won't do you much good. To this end, we recommend strategies like finding an accountability partner, establishing a rewards system, and creating goal reminders. If you have already thought about the emotional motivation behind your goals and taken the time to envision your future, you are likely already motivated to achieve your goals. But these strategies can help you make sure you stay focused on them.

Secondly, it can be difficult to stay organized and break your long-term goals down into short-term goals you can work on each day. To help you keep your momentum going and make progress through completing small, manageable tasks, we offer suggestions like keeping a goals journal and creating detailed to-do lists. You should already have broken your goals into manageable steps as part of your action plan, but working on your goals journal and your to-do lists can help you stay focused on the small steps you need to take to achieve the big payoff.

Paying attention to both aspects of your needs will help you better succeed. Although lots of other goal-setting guides or advice gurus act like there is one correct path to achieve success, this really isn't the case. Everyone is a little different. What works for one person may not work for another. So choose the methods that sound like they will work best for you based on your past experiences. And if they don't work, try something else until you find the right combination of strategies to keep you accountable and organized.

Goal Journal

By now you should have written out your goals as part of your action plan. You may have already noticed how powerful that feels. Something about putting your goals into words and committing those words to paper makes them start to feel more real. When you spell out your goals in writing, they start to feel like you are really going to achieve them.

Writing down your goals and creating a written action plan is obviously the first, important step you must take towards achieving any goals. But journaling about the process of trying to achieve those goals has many additional benefits. Journaling can help keep you accountable for your progress, by forcing you to stop and reflect on your goal progress each day. This reflection can also help you clarify your goals or make any needed adjustments to your goal timeline or strategy.

You can use any kind of notebook or journal for your goals journal. A slightly larger journal is better so you have more room to write. However, if you find goal journaling especially useful and want to start carrying a smaller journal around with you during the day, that would be a great idea.

You can also use a digital journal by taking notes into a Word document or using a private or public journal on a website like Tumblr, Livejournal, or others. If you know you spend more time online than offline, a digital journal might make more sense. But if you go this route, you also should spend some time journaling on paper, as writing your goals out by hand will help you set your intentions more powerfully.

The first section of your goal journal should be your action plan. Detailing your visions of the future, your specific goals, and the shorter tasks those goals are broken into is the first step of any goal-setting process. You should keep this action plan close at hand in your goal journal so it is easy to refer back to.

When you are first getting started with a new goal or with goal-setting in general, it is important to make your goals not just a long-term project, but a series of daily tasks. To that end, you should take notes in your goals journal every single day for at least the first month of your new, goal-oriented life. Your daily entries can be very brief. Simply note down whether or not you stayed focused on your goals during the day and write down any specific tasks you have achieved.

Once a week, you should write a more comprehensive entry. You should detail what tasks you have achieved as well as any obstacles you faced along the way. If you struggled to stay focused on your goals or meet your short-term goals for the week, write a little bit about why that happened. Don't be too hard on yourself; simply explain what happened so you can start to figure out how to keep it from happening again.

In monthly entries, you should similarly reflect on how your goals are progressing in the longer term. If you did well three weeks out of the month but struggled one week, first pat yourself on the back for your success, then think about why your failures happened. Maybe the pace you set for yourself was unreasonable and lightening your load would make it easier to achieve everything. Feel free to make adjustments to your plans for the next month based on your successes or difficulties this month. As before, don't judge yourself or be hard on yourself for how things are going; simply figure out how to ensure your success down the line.

If keeping a goal journal sounds like more work than it is worth, feel free to use some combination of other methods to keep you accountable and focused. Regardless of whether you are using this method formally or not, however, you should still check in with yourself on your goal progress regularly, even if you do this in a less formal way. Reflecting on your goal progress in whatever form is one of the best ways to ensure you stay focused and on track.

To-Do Lists

Another useful technique for achieving your goals is one you might already be familiar with: creating to-do lists. Although your action plan is like one, long to-do list, you can also use to-do lists on a more daily basis to help you be sure you are staying focused and achieving your goals.

You can keep your to-do lists in as simple or as complicated a way as you like. You can use a simple pen and paper for your to-do list or a dedicated notebook. You also might incorporate a to-do list section into your goal-setting journal, if you are keeping one, or you could use a large paper calendar. You can also use a digital to-do list, which we'll talk about more in the next paragraph. Use whatever form for your to-do lists that you think you are most likely to use.

If you want to use an online or computer platform for your to-do lists, there are an assortment of websites that work. If you use Microsoft Outlook on your work or home computers, you may already be familiar with this program's to-do list features. You can also use websites like Remember the Milk, Google Tasks, Todoist, Ta-Da Lists, or Toodledo. Just search the names of any of these websites to take advantage of them. If you use a smartphone or tablet, there are also an array of apps that can be used to keep your to-do lists organized. Evernote is one popular app that can be used to create and organize to-do lists related to a variety of goals. OneNote, Remember the Milk, Google Tasks, and Wunderlist all come highly recommended from PCWorld.com. Many of these apps allow you to integrate your to-do list with your laptop or desktop computer, so you can check things off no matter where you are working. If you spend a lot of time looking at your devices or worry that you would not remember to consult a paper to-do list, try to incorporate your goals into your digital life. If you prefer a paper list or find this kind of technology a hassle, however, feel free to stick with the pen and pad.

Whatever platform you decide to use, you should consult your to-do lists every day, but you should outline your tasks by the week. Your goals for the week, based on the timeline for your milestones, can be broken down into daily tasks. You should take time one day per week to dole out the tasks you need to achieve each day to reach your weekly goals. Setting out your to-do list tasks by the week is better than doing it by the day, because doing it by the week helps you make sure you don't procrastinate. You can spread things out fairly evenly, or you can allot differing numbers of tasks to different days based on what else is going on in your life. Setting out your tasks each week can also help you make sure you take advantage of your time. If you find extra time on Tuesday, you can get started on Wednesday's tasks, rather than wasting your time watching extra TV.

Whatever platform you are using, you should be sure to include a variety of tasks when you are creating your daily to-do lists. Try to include several tasks you could complete quickly, mixed in with tasks that might take longer or be more difficult. Also be sure to break large tasks into smaller ones, especially if the task seems daunting. If your goal for the day is to learn to play a new song on the guitar, you might break it down like this:

- Browse and choose a song to play.
- Look up any unfamiliar chords in the song and practice making their shapes.
- Learn to play the chords to the verses.
- Learn to play the chords to the chorus.
- Play the song through slowly five times.
- Play the song through at proper tempo ten times.

Now, rather than feeling daunted by seeing "Learn to play a new song" on your list, you will be able to accomplish each achievable task. Some of these tasks will only take ten or fifteen minutes, so those will be easy to achieve. This can help you stay motivated and build your momentum over the day, rather than feeling daunted by what you have to do.

Furthermore, you want your to-do list to help you feel like you are getting things done. If it will take you the better part of the day to achieve your ultimate goal, don't make yourself wait all day to get the satisfaction of crossing something off. Also, maybe you don't quite get to the point where you'd cross off "Learn to play a new song" from your list, but you complete steps 1-5. You deserve to give yourself credit for all your hard work along the way, even if you still need to put in a little more work before you can cross off that ultimate goal.

To the end of using your to-do list to help you feel like you are getting things done all day, you should also incorporate a mix of different kinds of tasks. If your major goal for the day is to "learn to play a new song," but you also need to practice some of your older pieces, or catch up on some emails, you should add those things in too. That way, if you need to take a break from your primary task, you can still feel like you are getting things done and working towards your big picture goal, which might be to become a successful musician.

If you know you are someone who is stressed out by having a big to-do list, feel free to use some combination of other methods instead. Do keep in mind, however, that your goals will need to be broken into smaller, daily tasks regardless, and that a to-do list can be one of the best ways to ensure that you make your goals manageable.

Creating Vision Boards

If you are a more visually-oriented person, you might also like to create a visual representation of your visions of the future. A vision board is a collage of images that represent your future life and goals. A vision board doesn't have to be particularly artistic, but creating one can be a chance to express your vision for the future in a creative way.

A vision board is a great way to help you clarify your visions of the future, especially if you are a more visual learner or visually-oriented person. A vision board can take what just seem like words or ideas and make them a more tangible reality. The process of creating a vision board can also be a relaxing and fun way to think about and clarify your goals. Also, having a vision board hanging up in a place where you see it, perhaps near your desk or in your bedroom, can help you stay focused and motivated to achieve your goals.

To make a vision board, you can use a sheet of poster board—which can be found at any craft or office supply store—as the basis for your board and cover it with images that represent your future life. You can find pictures in magazines, newspapers, or on the Internet and cut and glue them to the board. You should create one for each of the stages of your life you explored in the "Visualizing the Future" exercises from the section on identifying your goals: ten years from now, five years from now, one year from now, and tomorrow. Try to make a visually pleasing arrangement, but don't worry if it doesn't look like a masterpiece. The goal is simply to collect images that you like that represent the kind of life you want to live and the kind of person you want to be.

The Internet and technology can also be useful tools to help you create your vision boards. You can use Google Image search to find pictures you can then print and affix to your boards. You also can use an online tool like Pinterest or Tumblr to create a virtual vision board. You can use these sites to find and organize images that represent your visions of the future. You can then refer back to your page on these sites to remind yourself of what kind of life you want to live. It's a good idea still to print out at least several images from your virtual boards and hang them in your physical space to use as reminders to stay motivated.

If the idea of cutting out and gluing pictures is not appealing to you, however, feel free to skip creating these boards. The vision board is simply a visual supplement that can motivate you as you go through this process.

Accountability Partners

Did your mother ever tell you, "You are who you surround yourself with?" Although she might have been warning you against surrounding yourself with bad influences, the same principle is true of good influences too. If you are motivated to achieve your goals, you need to surround yourself with motivated people.

Now, you might not be able to do a complete overhaul of your friends and family, but you certainly can find one person who can become a good influence on your goals. This person can become your "accountability partner." Having an accountability partner who will keep you focused on your goals will make you more likely to stay on track and successfully achieve them.

Most of us can be pretty motivated by facing shame or embarrassment, so having an accountability partner who you have to report back to each week can be a good kick in the pants to make sure you don't have to report failing to meet your goals. Your accountability partner can also be a great cheerleader, someone to help keep you motivated and remind you of why you are setting out on this goal journey in the first place. Also, having someone else trying to tackle a similar big task or obstacle can help you feel less alone. If other people in your life are not as motivated as you, it can make it feel like you are putting all this work in for nothing. An accountability partner can remind you that your work and effort are worthwhile and that you're not alone in your desire to make positive change in your life.

The first thing you have to do to use this method is find the person who will become your accountability partner. Even if family, friends, or a romantic partner are not working towards similar goals to yours, you can surely find someone else in your life who is looking to improve himself or herself, build a business, or make a change in his or her life. It doesn't matter if you are working towards the same goals; what is important is that you both want to set goals and make change. You should find be a person you are comfortable being honest with, but it does not have to be a close personal friend or family member. In fact, it is sometimes easier to be honest with someone who is a little separate from the rest of your personal life.

It might seem a bit awkward at first to ask someone to enter into this kind of relationship with you, but trust that this person will be benefitting as much as you, so you shouldn't worry about imposing. You can send this person an e-mail or bring up the question in person. And if the first person you approach turns you down, don't get discouraged. Simply try another person. Maybe you can think of a whole group of people who might make sense as an accountability group. If so, feel free to establish accountability relationships with multiple people. Just make sure that everyone is on the same page and equally dedicated to keeping each other accountable and motivated.

Once you have found the person who will become your accountability partner, you should set up a regular meeting time. You could meet in person at a coffee shop, in the break room at work if you work together, or at one of your homes. Choose a place where both of you can concentrate, relax, and talk comfortably. You could also set a weekly time to meet over a video chatting program like Skype, Google Hangout, or Facetime. E-mail or phone conversations can work also, but it is better to interact face-to-face if possible. Allot yourself at least half an hour for each meeting, though you can meet for longer, especially if you end up socializing in addition to talking about your goals.

It is important that you establish a regular meeting time. A once per week meeting is ideal. If that's not possible, it can work to meet face-to-face every other week or even once per month, though you should supplement with weekly check-ins over e-mail or phone. Whatever schedule you decide upon, it is essential that your meetings fall on a regular schedule that you both stick to.

At your first meeting, you should each spend time explaining exactly what your goals are. Show your accountability partner your action plan and explain to him or her your goals and your vision for the future. Show them what the timeline for your goals looks like, taking note of any important way stations or milestones along the way. Make a copy of your action plan, or share a digital document with your accountability partner so they can see what your timeline is like. You should also talk about what you hope your accountability partner will do for you, what kinds of motivation or support you might need.

Then, before each future meeting, you should each spend a little time taking notes or reflecting on your goal progress since the time you last met. The whole point of your accountability partner is to keep you honest and accountable, so be completely truthful. If you had a bad week and didn't get anything done, be prepared to own up to it. When you meet, you should share your notes and explain your successes and your failures. If you achieved all your goals for the week, talk about why. If you didn't, also try and talk about why. See if your accountability partner has any suggestions for ways to do things differently this week so you can have greater success.

There are other ways you can use your accountability partnership too, depending on your particular goals. If you have creative goals like writing, you can set up a day each week when you have to send your accountability partner some of your work. The point isn't to worry about whether the work is good or not or to ask your accountability partner for comments; the most important thing is just pushing the work through to completion because you know someone will be expecting to see it. The same can be true if you are drafting a business plan, creating a website, learning web design, or working on many other goals.

If you know you are more of a loner or

can't find anyone in your life who would make a good accountability partner, this method might not be the best for you. If you do find the right person, however, having someone else involved in helping you achieve your goals can make all the difference between goals that get abandoned and goals that you follow through to completion.

Goal Reminders

One of the hardest things when you are first getting started with your goals is making them a part of your daily life. Especially if your goals are things you may have been putting off working towards for a long time, you may be used to disregarding them in your daily life.

To get you focused on your goals, you may want to incorporate physical or digital reminders. These reminders should just be something left in a place where you'll see it in your daily routine to remind you of your goals. The note might just say "Stay Positive" or "Keep Focused" or could say something specific you want to remember to work on. Physical reminders could be something like Post-its or other notes hung in visible places in your house that remind you to keep your goals in mind. Good places for these reminders are on mirrors, in your doorway, on your desk, or on an interior door. You could also incorporate this kind of reminder in your digital life. You could change your computer desktop text or screensaver text or add something to the background of your cell phone. The point of these reminders is just to help you keep your goals in mind during points in your day when you might otherwise forget about them.

You can also use digital or paper calendars to remind you of your goals. A digital calendar like Google's Calendar application can be used to keep your goal timelines and deadlines organized. This calendar (and others online) can also be used to send e-mail or text message reminders of approaching deadlines. Whether you use a paper or digital calendar, you probably already mark out times for appointments, meetings, and other deadlines on these calendars. Your goal deadlines and the time you will dedicate to achieving your goals should also have a place on your schedule, as these deadlines are just as important.

Another way to use a paper calendar is to take a tip from comedian Jerry Seinfeld. When Jerry Seinfeld's show *Seinfeld* was first getting started, he told a young aspiring comedian that his advice for becoming a better comedian was simple: to become a better comedian, you have to write every day. And to make sure that this happened, Jerry Seinfeld would hang a large paper calendar in his apartment, in a highly visible place. His calendar was actually the whole year on one very large page, but you could also do something similar with large monthly calendars. Then, for each day that he spent time writing jokes, he would put a big red X on that date on the calendar. Watching the calendar fill with red X's is a great motivator, and Seinfeld emphasized that you should "not break the chain" of Xs. Whatever your goal is, marking off days when you complete goal-related tasks can be a very good motivator to help you build momentum.

These goal reminders are most important during the first month or two of working towards a new goal because it takes at least a month for something to become a habit. Reminders can help you establish a habit of working towards your goals, so that in the future you won't even need to be reminded.

Rewards System

When you reach the final stage of achieving a goal, you finally get the payoff you have been working towards. You get the feeling of satisfaction of achieving your goal, and you also get to see the rewards of your hard work: a new job, a healthier body, a better relationship, or whatever the goal is. However, many of us need smaller rewards or incentives to keep us motivated along the way.

A recent study from the Mayo Clinic has shown that financial incentives actually help people achieve their weight loss goals. In the study, participants were encouraged to lose four pounds per month. One group of participants was in a group set up to receive incentives, while the other was in a group that received no incentives. For participants in the incentive group, if they met their goal, they received $20.00, while if they didn't meet their goal, they had to pay $20.00 into a group pool. The other participants received no incentives for meeting their weight loss goals.

The results showed that 62% of the participants in the incentive group met their goal, compared to only 26% in the non-incentive group. The participants in the incentive group lost an average of close to 9 pounds, while the participants in the non-incentive group averaged only 2 pounds. These startling numbers show the power of incentives, even relatively small ones, for helping you stay motivated to achieve your goals.

Of course, we all do this on a smaller scale too. When you finish a project at work, you may reward yourself with a snack or with a stroll around the office. When you finish doing housework, you may reward yourself with an hour of TV or a piece of dessert. Incentives like these can be incorporated into your goal-setting action plan.

If you want to use incentives to help motivate you to achieve your goals, you want to pick an incentive that will work for you. Financial incentives can be highly motivating for a variety of goals. If you are lucky enough to find someone who is willing to spend his or her money to motivate you for your goals, that might be the ideal situation. However, you can also dedicate a certain amount of your own money to serving as a goal incentive. You could make yourself pay penalty money to a friend or send it to a charity you don't particularly want to support.

If your goals are financially-motivated already, if you don't have excess money to use as a motivator, or if you simply don't think you'd find money to be an effective motivator, you could think of a different rewards system to motivate you. For achieving short-term, daily goals, you could reward yourself with a guilty-pleasure relaxation activity like watching a favorite TV show, playing a video game, or having a glass of wine. For longer term goals, you could award yourself a small vacation, a shopping trip at the mall, or a long weekend off just to relax as rewards for achieving significant milestones along the way to your goal. It's important that your goal rewards be things you wouldn't usually let yourself do or have, but pretty much anything that works to motivate you is fair game for a rewards system.

Although it can work to be in control of your own rewards system, it can be more effective and motivating to put control in someone else's hands. If you have an accountability partner, as explained earlier in this section, your accountability partner can be in charge of doling out your incentives when you achieve a milestone or simply stay on track, whatever system you wish to put in place. Even if you don't have an accountability partner, you can probably find someone in your life who can keep money put aside for you to be given out only when you demonstrate a certain amount of progress. If your reward is a special snack or activity, someone else could keep the keys to the cupboard or the password to the Tivo from you until you achieve your goal.

Of course, if you have willpower enough of your own, feel free to be in charge of your own rewards system. But it will work best if you truly penalize yourself for failing to meet your goals. So no cheating!

Overcoming Roadblocks

If you have tried and failed to achieve some of the goals you are now thinking about, you may be starting to worry about what to do when life just gets in the way. This is, of course, sometimes inevitable. Changes in your home life, unexpected health issues, or being laid off from your job are among some of the many potential disruptions that could get in the way of you achieving your goals.

This section will provide some guidelines and advice for coping with life's roadblocks, as well as some tips for pushing through a slump or low motivation. This advice, combined with the methods for achieving your goals outlined in the previous chapter, should help you overcome any obstacles you encounter along the road to goal success.

Staying Focused on Your Goals

It is hard to think of wiser words than those of poet Robert Burns: "The best laid schemes of mice and men often go awry." This quote speaks to the sometimes inevitable disruptions to daily life that are outside of our control. These disruptions can threaten your progress towards your goals, but not if you have some methods for coping with them.

Perhaps in the past you have set out to

achieve a goal like losing weight or learning a new skill, only to find yourself abandoning the goal when some outside difficulty in another part of your life appeared. Learning how to be prepared for and cope with these kinds of outside influences is crucial if you want to see your goals come to completion.

First, it is essential that you make your goal work part of a regular, ideally daily, habit. Daily habits are hard to disrupt. Only in the worst circumstances will you let habits like brushing your teeth, drinking your morning coffee, or even checking Facebook slide. The same will be true if you make working on your goals a daily habit. You won't even think of skipping out on working towards your goals if you make it as much of a natural part of your routine as eating breakfast or turning on the television. To this end, you should be using the activities outlined in the previous section to make your goal work a daily habit. This is most important in the first month of working towards a new goal, as studies have shown that it takes 21 consecutive days of doing something to establish a habit. A firmly entrenched habit will not be so easily interrupted by life's comings and goings.

Additionally, doing the work of setting up a goal, creating an action plan, and starting to carry out the plan should hopefully have reminded you what is important to you in life. There are plenty of little things that can crop up in a day that can threaten to take you off course, but if you know that your goals are the most important thing, you should carry that attitude with you even when things get tough. You know that your goals are important to you and that working towards them every day is the only way to achieve them in the long term. So when something else comes up that seems like it needs more of your attention, re-visit your visions of the future. Envision what it will look like when you achieve your goal and don't let any passing distraction, no matter how pressing it may seem, keep you from reaching that future.

Also, keep perspective on the relationship between short-term crises and long-term problems. Many short-term problems require long-term solutions. A short-term financial crisis can only really be fixed by adjusting the underlying long-term financial issues. You may need to do something immediately to alleviate the crisis, but to keep it from happening again, you may need to achieve your goal of long term financial stability. Similarly, a health crisis you experience now may be related to your long-term health goals. Of course, this isn't always the case, as life stressors can come in from completely outside your control, but sometimes focusing on the long-term *is* addressing the short term, so it is important to stay focused on your long-term goals.

If you establish a habit of working on

your goals and make a commitment to creating time and space for goal work in your life, you will find it easier to deal with life's obstacles and difficulties. Again, the most crucial time for establishing a habit is the first month or two. If it feels difficult to focus on your goals during this first month, push through and rest assured that it will become easier over time, no matter what life throws your way.

Forgiving Yourself

I have this friend; let's call her Kelly. Kelly is always saying how she wants to lose weight and it seems like every time I see her she has come up with a new system for losing the weight she wants to lose. She's joined a gym, signed up for Weight Watchers, or started a juice diet. She sets up her goals and develops a plan for her life, then gets going and has a good week or two.

Then she slips up. She has a bad day and just can't resist a slice of chocolate cake. Or she's exhausted driving home from work and pulls through the McDonald's drive-through. Or she misses a week of working out because she comes down with a cold. Next thing you know, Kelly is beating herself up so badly about messing up that she's back to her old habits. It's her negative self-image that is keeping her in her unhealthy habits and that unravels her efforts to lose weight.

Here's the thing: slip-ups are inevitable, especially when you are working towards a goal that forces you to change some long-held habits. Even if your goal isn't about changing a habit but is instead about learning a skill or moving up professionally, you are still going to slip up sometimes. You are going to have a crummy day and just not feel like working towards your goals. When this happens, the worst thing you can do is beat yourself up about it. Telling yourself you are worthless and that your goals are not worth pursuing will only help you fall back into an old cycle or put your goals on the backburner.

Instead, you should focus on forgiving yourself. Although you of course want to keep working towards your goals every day and should push yourself to do so, if it's too late to do any goal work for the day or if you've gone off track with a diet or exercise plan, there's nothing you can do to change it. Better to simply forgive yourself and move on.

It can also be a good idea to prepare for this day by having a slip-up plan. If you are working with an accountability partner, be prepared to explain to your partner that you had a rough day or week. You should talk through what happened and see if you can find a way to avoid a similar kind of day in the future. Maybe you want to get your goal work done earlier in the day so you don't get too worn out to do it. Maybe you need to have some back-up healthy meals in the freezer for nights you are too tired to cook. Maybe you were just asking yourself to do more than was reasonable in one day and that made you feel so overwhelmed that you did nothing at all. If possible, adjust your strategy in response to the slip-up so that you can get back on track with a better success rate.

You could also try writing yourself a little note in the event of a slip-up. This note should remind you of why you are setting out on this goal journey and speak kindly to yourself in spite of the mistakes you may have made.

> **Try it Now:** Writing a slip-up note can be a great exercise in self-forgiveness, even if you don't end up having to use it. Write a letter to yourself in the future after you have slipped up or lost sight of your goals for some length of time. Keep the tone kind but firm. Write it like you were speaking to a friend or loved one who came to you after having a similar kind of slip-up on the way to focusing on their goals. Include a description of why you are setting out to achieve this goal and what the emotional motivation behind it us. Remind yourself why this goal matters and describe the positive results that will come about after achieving it.

Tell your future self that you forgive him or her and that all that matters is getting back on track starting right away. After you write this note, you should keep it in your goal journal or give it to your accountability partner to give to you in the event that you need it.

If you find yourself slipping up often or struggling to establish your goal work into a new habit, you might try using some different tools and strategies for incorporating your goals into your life. If you were using goal reminders and keeping a goal journal but don't have an accountability partner, maybe try to find one. If you have an accountability partner and a rewards system but aren't using goal reminders to keep you focused in your physical space, maybe try creating some of those too. There's no one-size-fits-all method, so keep experimenting until you reach the right balance of accountability and motivation.

Adapting Goals to Changes

Let's say you set a goal for yourself to lose fifty pounds over the course of the next year. You start off strong, losing weight at a healthy rate, but soon you start to plateau. Nothing you try to jumpstart your weight loss seems to be working, so you go to see a doctor. The doctor diagnoses you with a thyroid condition that is going to make weight loss at the rate you had originally intended impossible. Obviously, the best response to this kind of change in your situation is to adapt your plans. Maybe you can only plan on losing twenty-five pounds next year, and will re-assess to see if it's possible to lose the next twenty-five the following year. Maybe it's not possible to lose those fifty pounds at all, but you can adapt different health goals to focus on establishing a healthier diet and exercise routine even without weight loss.

Obviously, when faced with an insurmountable obstacle like this one, you have to adapt. Unfortunately, you might face similar, if less obvious, obstacles along the way to achieving your goals, obstacles that really can't just be overcome or worked through. If you experience a loss in your family, a financial hardship, or even just the stress of having to move, change jobs, or adapt to a new health issue, your goals in related or unrelated areas might need to be changed as well.

While you want to prioritize your goals and stick through them in spite of difficulties or challenges, it is also okay to change or abandon a goal if it no longer makes sense. There is a difference between having a hard time staying focused on your goals and facing a legitimate roadblock that forces you to re-assess. In the example above, if you were simply struggling to stick to your diet and exercise routine, that might be cause to re-visit your emotional motivation for achieving your goal or try new methods for staying motivated, but not a good reason to abandon your goal altogether. On the other hand, you might need to put your goals on hold if you were failing to meet your goal deadlines because you were laid off from your job and need to spend your time job-hunting or because you have had to take on new caretaker duties for an ailing family member.

Whenever possible though, you should try to stick to your goals, even if you need to modify your timeline for goal completion. If a major life event takes place that requires more of your immediate attention, maybe pause your goal progression for several weeks or a month or else re-distribute the events on your timeline based on a new, lessened weekly time commitment. It is important that you regularly check in on your goal progress so that you can identify if a problem like this is coming up. If you are falling behind, you need to consider whether your timeline should be modified or if you need to change your approach in some way.

If you are feeling down about having to adapt or abandon a goal, don't despair. You should consider goal-setting a lifelong process. The skills you have learned in this book should be used to help you achieve whatever goals you need to set. You should not fixate on achieving one particular goal at the exclusion of realistically considering your needs and priorities. Your goal-setting aims will change, but the skills you use to achieve your goals will only become stronger as you achieve more and develop new interests and objectives.

Don't be afraid of change. The most successful people are those who learn the skills they need to overcome and work with whatever life throws at them. Think of an obstacle or a change in your life as an opportunity to re-assess your current goals and possibly develop new ones in response. This isn't a bad thing. Sometimes hardships help us realize our true priorities and help us focus on our goals with new energy. We just have to be open to the re-evaluations that may come about as a result of that change.

Conclusion

Now that you have read through this book, you should be ready to set out on your first goal journey. You should know exactly where you are headed and why you want to go there, what route you will take and what milestones you will achieve along the way, and what strategies you will use to make your trip a successful one. You should also have some ideas for how to cope with unexpected roadblocks or obstacles that you may encounter once you are on the road.

The tools you learn to set and achieve one goal successfully can be directly translated to all of your future goals. Remember that it's normal for this first goal to feel like the hardest one, because you might need to break some old habits and set some new ones in order to achieve it. The methods described in this book should help you be able to successfully push through to achieve your first goal, and this success will set you up for many more successfully-completed goals in the future.

Also, you should consult our free, downloadable goal-setting worksheets (accessible here: http://empowermentnation.com/downloads/38/GoalsettingWorksheet.pdf) to use as a template for each goal action plan and to organize and summarize your overall goals for the future. These worksheets can be incorporated with your other goal journaling or to-do lists, or can be printed out and hung up to serve as goal reminders.

So start opening up your maps, packing up your trunk, and getting ready for the road ahead. You are on the road to success, whatever and wherever that means for you.

**Visit
EmpowermentNation.com
to view other fantastic books and to
sign up for book alerts, giveaways,
and updates!**

www.ingramcontent.com/pod-product-compliance
Lightning Source LLC
Chambersburg PA
CBHW071802200526
45167CB00017B/994